KANE BROWN

TWO EXTRAORDINARY PEOPLE.

SAM HUNT

CONNECTED LIVES™

Ariana Grande | Camila Cabello

Ed Sheeran | Shawn Mendes

Halsey | Billie Eilish

John Legend | Michael Bublé

Kacey Musgraves | Maren Morris

Kane Brown | Sam Hunt

Kendrick Lamar | Travis Scott

Nicki Minaj | Cardi B

Photo credits: page 4: Kevin Winter via Getty Images; page 5: Kevin Winter / Stagecoach via Getty Images; page 6: James Crittenden / EyeEm via Getty Images; page 7: DemureDragonfly / iStock via Getty Images; page 8: Ethan Miller via Getty Images; page 9: Cooper Neill / iHeartMedia via Getty Images, mf-guddyx / E+ via Getty Images; page 10: Kevin Winter / dcp via Getty Images; page 11: Michael Ochs Archives via Getty Images; page 12: groveb / E+ via Getty Images, Rick Kern / iHeartMedia via Getty Images; page 13: Frederick M. Brown via Getty Images; page 16: Brian Ach / Something in the Water via Getty Images; page 17: Ethan Miller / iHeartMedia via Getty Images; page 18: Maskot via Getty Images, Jason Kempin via Getty Images; page 20: Frederick M. Brown via Getty Images; page 21: Alberto E. Rodriguez via Getty Images; page 23: Kevin Winter / iHeartMedia via Getty Images; page 24: CarlaMc / iStock via Getty Images, Rick Diamond / Kicker Country Stampede via Getty Images; page 25: Mike Zarrilli via Getty Images; page 28: Jason Kempin via Getty Images; page 29: Ethan Miller via Getty Images; page 31: Kevin Winter via Getty Images; page 32: Kevork Djansezian / dcp via Getty Images, Brian Ach / YouTube via Getty Images; page 33: Rick Diamond / Kicker Country Stampede via Getty Images; page 34: Ethan Miller / iHeartMedia via Getty Images; page 35: Daniel Boczarski / Windy City Smokeout via Getty Images; page 37: Rick Diamond / Kicker Country Stampede via Getty Images; page 40: Joel Carillet / iStock Unreleased via Getty Images; page 41: Ethan Miller via Getty Images; page 43: David Redfern / Redferns via Getty Images; page 46: Anna Webber / CMT via Getty Images; page 47: Rick Diamond / CMT via Getty Images; page 48: Rick Diamond / CMT via Getty Images; page 49: Jason Kempin / CMT via Getty Images; page 50: Photo by Matthew Simmons / dcp via Getty Images; page 51: Anna Webber / CMT via Getty Images; page 52: Frederick Breedon IV / Country Music Hall of Fame and Museum via Getty Images; page 53: Kevin Winter / Stagecoach via Getty Images; page 55: Jason Kempin via Getty Images; page 56: Jason Kempin / CMT via Getty Images; page 57: Maury Phillips / ASCAP via Getty Images; page 59: Frazer Harrison / ACM via Getty Images; page 62: Rick Diamond / Pepsi's Rock The South via Getty Images; page 63: Rick Diamond via Getty Images; page 64: Kevin Winter / dcp via Getty Images, Kevin Winter / Stagecoach via Getty Images; background: Chris Wong / EyeEm via Getty Images; Kane Brown head shot: Frazer Harrison via Getty Images; Sam Hunt head shot: Michael Loccisano / CMT via Getty Images

ISBN: 978-1-68021-790-2
eBook: 978-1-64598-076-6

Printed in Malaysia

24 23 22 21 20   1 2 3 4 5

TABLE OF CONTENTS

CHAPTER 1

EARLY LIFE

WHO IS KANE BROWN?

Kane Brown is a social media star and country singer. He was born on October 21, 1993, in Chattanooga, Tennessee. His mother is Tabatha Brown. She raised him on her own. Growing up, Kane didn't know his father. Moving around was normal to Kane as a child. The small family lived in several different towns in Georgia and Tennessee. For a while, they lived on a farm. It belonged to Kane's grandfather.

WHO IS SAM HUNT?

Sam Hunt was born on December 8, 1984, in Cedartown, Georgia. He is a country music singer and songwriter. His parents, Joan and Allen, raised him. Joan was a third-grade teacher. Allen worked as an insurance agent. Ben and Van are Sam's younger brothers. Sam spent his whole childhood in the same town. This was very different from Kane's experience.

A DIFFICULT CHILDHOOD

Childhood wasn't easy for Kane. He grew up in poverty. "I had a single mom. She was 18 when she had me. She didn't have a job at all," he told an audience in Texas. The two moved often. This meant Kane had to change schools too. At times, Kane and his mom didn't have anywhere to live. Sometimes they had to sleep in their car. It was hard to find cheap housing.

LIFE IN THE COUNTRY

Sam's hometown is small. It has around 10,000 people. Most of his relatives lived within 10 minutes of him. "It's the kind of town that everybody knows everybody," he told Vevo Lift. While growing up, Sam hunted in the woods with his family. He also enjoyed fishing. The brothers played sports outside their family home. Baseball, football, and basketball were favorites. "I was always out in the yard playing," Sam said.

GETTING BULLIED

When Kane was in middle school, kids bullied him. The singer is biracial. His mother is white, and his father is African American and Cherokee. He explained to *People* magazine, "I didn't know that until I was seven or eight years old." Classmates started calling him names. He tried to ignore them. "I kept my circle small. I had my friends that I knew wouldn't do anything to hurt me."

COUNTRY KID

Sam grew up in a rural area. He spent a lot of time outside with his brothers and friends. Riding horses was one of his favorite activities. As a kid, he got a horse for Christmas. One of his childhood dreams was to join the rodeo. The brothers used to pretend they were riding bulls. Once, Sam even put his younger brother Van on the family goat.

FAMILY HELP

Sometimes Kane lived with his grandmother in Georgia. Nana helped raise him. She was a good role model. For a while, Nana worked as a detective. While his grandmother worked, Kane got to hang out at the police station.

Another important person was Kane's great-grandfather. Papa owned a store called the Cold Spot in Rossville, Georgia. When Kane was living there, he would visit the shop after school. The store was a stable part of his life.

STORYTELLING

Sam's family liked to go dove hunting. They would leave in the morning before the sun was up. Sam, his brothers, and their grandfather wanted to be in place early. Everyone would settle into their spots. Then they had to wait. Half an hour before sunrise was when hunting could start. This was the law. To pass the time, their grandfather told them stories. Sam loved listening. Telling stories would become an important part of his own life.

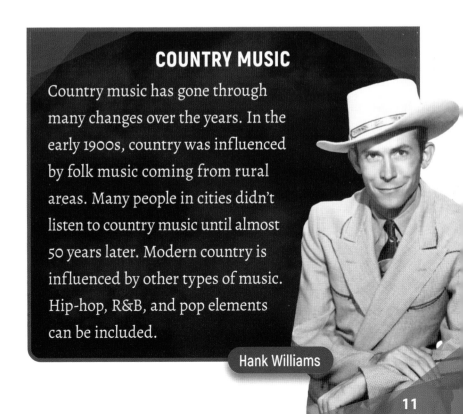

COUNTRY MUSIC

Country music has gone through many changes over the years. In the early 1900s, country was influenced by folk music coming from rural areas. Many people in cities didn't listen to country music until almost 50 years later. Modern country is influenced by other types of music. Hip-hop, R&B, and pop elements can be included.

Hank Williams

SPORTS TALENT

Kane started playing sports at age three. By high school, he had been a quarterback on the football team and captain of the basketball team. He was a pitcher in baseball too. Sports came naturally to him. "I was always one of the best players on the team," he told *People*. As a child, Kane never imagined he would become a country star. His family thought he would become an athlete.

FOOTBALL STAR

Just like Kane, Sam had not thought about a career in music. Sports were what he wanted to do. His parents supported this dream. "Music was something I had never been encouraged [to do] in that way," he told fans at a concert. In high school, he played football, basketball, and baseball. Sam was especially good at football. He was named the Co-Offensive Player of the Year by his hometown newspaper. This was in 2002.

FROM ATHLETE TO MUSICIAN

Many country music stars played sports before going into music. Brian Kelley from the group Florida Georgia Line played baseball. He was on the Florida State University team before becoming a star. Chase Rice was a linebacker for the University of North Carolina. Like Sam, he also started playing the guitar in college. Lee Brice played football at Clemson University until he injured his arm. The discipline he had learned from sports helped him in his music career.

Brian Kelley

WHAT NEXT?

Kane's family moved around a lot. Because of this, he went to five different high schools. After graduating, Kane wanted to join the Army. There was only one problem. He had tattoos. The Army said these would have to be removed. Kane didn't want to do that. Instead, he got a job at FedEx. During this time, Kane made videos of himself singing. It began as something to do for fun. Soon, it would become more than that.

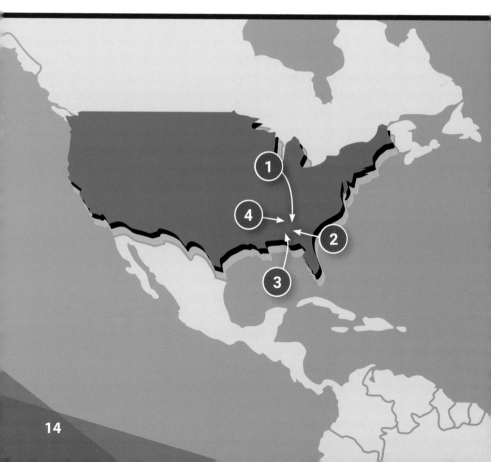

COLLEGE YEARS

Sam went a different route after high school. Middle Tennessee State University recruited him in 2003. They wanted him to play football. During his first year, the quarterback didn't play in any games. The next year, he only played in six. In 2005, Sam transferred to the University of Alabama at Birmingham (UAB). There, he was a starting quarterback. During his free time, he played the guitar.

KANE BROWN

1. **Fort Oglethorpe, Georgia:** Kane sang in the school choir and met Lauren Alaina, who would later support his music.

2. **Rossville, Georgia:** His great-grandfather's store, the Cold Spot, was here.

SAM HUNT

3. **Montevallo, Alabama:** Sam named his first album after this town.

4. **Nashville, Tennessee:** Moving here was Sam's first big step in his professional music career.

CHAPTER 2

INTRO TO MUSIC

R&B ROOTS

During middle school, Kane discovered R&B music. Two of his favorite musicians were Usher and Chris Brown. The teenager also liked country music. His mom and grandmother played country music nonstop. "My mom, my nana, my aunt raised me, so I was raised by all women, listening to Shania Twain, Sugarland—all female artists," he said on *Entertainment Tonight*. Later, he wanted to explore other country artists.

Usher

TURN UP THE RADIO

Sam loved listening to music on the radio. He would borrow his mom's keys and sit in her car in the driveway. Country music played on the car radio for hours.

In high school, Sam listened to rap and rock music with his football team. They always had music playing in the locker room. This music made them more energetic on the field.

FORCED TO SING

When Kane was 13, he started going to a new middle school. It was in Fort Oglethorpe, Georgia. All students at the school were required to take choir. Kane didn't want to. Back then, sports were the only thing he wanted to do. However, he had no choice. The future star didn't know how important choir would turn out to be.

JUST A HOBBY

After high school, Sam listened to a friend play guitar. He decided to buy his own instrument. This was right before he started college. "I was a huge music fan, but I never understood playing an instrument," he told the *Daily Country*. Sam taught himself how to play the guitar. He also learned to sing. In the beginning, this was just a hobby. Classes and football practice kept him busy. Music was a way to relax.

TOOLS OF THE TRADE

Guitars play a big role in country music. Different kinds are used depending on what sound the artist wants. Traditional country music relies a lot on acoustic guitars. Electric guitars give country a more modern feel. Sometimes they add a rock 'n' roll element.

Many unique instruments also add to the sounds of country. String instruments like fiddles and banjos might be used. Banjos are played like a guitar. They have a circular body shape. Harmonicas and accordions can also be played.

A LITTLE ENCOURAGEMENT

When choir started, Kane sat in the back. He wouldn't sing with the others. One day, a girl in his class overheard him humming. She thought he sounded good. Lauren Alaina encouraged Kane to sing in class. The choir teacher heard them talking and asked him to sing. Kane's teacher was impressed. Alaina and Kane performed a duet. It wouldn't be their last.

HELP FROM HIS FRIENDS

Sam still didn't take music seriously in college. He explained to *Rolling Stone*, "Music is more of a . . . laid-back type, chilled-out kind of activity." Like Kane, he needed some encouragement to move to the next step. College friends and roommates heard Sam sing songs he had written. This impressed them. They encouraged him to start playing small gigs. When he was 21, he gave his first performance. It was at a small bar near UAB.

GAINING CONFIDENCE

Alaina's encouragement made Kane more comfortable with singing in choir. He still had to overcome his nerves about singing alone, though. "I'm shy offstage, but back then I was real shy anywhere," Kane told *Taste of Country*. His friends heard him singing to himself. It seemed like no one was paying attention. However, some people were.

MUSIC CITY, U.S.A.

Nashville, Tennessee, is the home of country music. It is known as Music City, U.S.A. Many people who want to work in country music move there. The city is full of producers, songwriters, singers, and musicians.

In the 1940s and 1950s, huge stars played there, including Elvis Presley. The city's popularity continued to grow. Some of today's biggest stars got their start in Nashville. Kelsea Ballerini and Taylor Swift were discovered there, among others.

WRITING MUSIC

Sam started to write his own music. One of his first songs was about his grandfather. "It was this little story about being young back where I was from," he said. One night he sang it for his college friends. He didn't know what they would think. The song was a big hit, so he continued to write. "I got a good reaction . . . and I kept doing it," he told *Hits Daily Double*.

TALENT SHOW

Kane was about to sing at a school talent show. His classmates expected him to sing an R&B or rap song. When he sang a country song, they were shocked. It was Chris Young's "Gettin' You Home." Some people booed at first. By the end, their reaction was different. Cheers rang out. Many yelled for Kane to sing again. Winning the contest made him think more about becoming a singer.

TRYING TO GO PRO

Even though he was writing his own music, Sam didn't plan on becoming a performer. He told the Boot, "It wasn't my dream to be a writer, an artist, for life." In college, sports were still his main focus. Sam was the starting quarterback for UAB. Trying to go pro seemed like the next step. In 2007, Sam graduated. A year later, he tried out for the Kansas City Chiefs. That plan didn't work out. Instead, Sam decided to try music.

Sam playing for the University of Alabama at Birmingham

POWER OF A CONCERT

Kane liked R&B. He loved the way Usher sang. However, the star's songs were too high-pitched for him. The deeper notes of country songs were a better fit for his baritone voice.

A friend bought tickets to a Brad Paisley and Chris Young concert. This was the first concert Kane went to. Seeing the stars perform was a turning point, he told the *Tennessean*. That's when an idea popped into his head. He thought, "I want to do this."

ON TO NASHVILLE

Writing music hadn't seemed like a job to Sam before. It was something he enjoyed as a hobby. Then he learned that Nashville was full of music publishers and producers. They worked with songwriters. Many had written hits that Sam had heard on the radio. Moving to Nashville was the next step. "I thought that I could have a career in music," he told AL.com. "I really didn't know exactly what I wanted to do or how I would go about doing it."

PARALLEL LIVES

Made music videos at home

Started singing in middle school

From the southern United States

Listened to country music growing up

Played football

Moved to Nashville to start his career

Started singing in college

CHAPTER 3

RISE TO SUCCESS

AN OLD FRIEND

Two important auditions were coming up for Kane. One was for *American Idol*. The other was for *The X Factor*. His middle school friend Lauren Alaina had made it onto *American Idol*. He had been shocked to see her on TV. Watching her made him want to audition. "She was a huge influence for me getting into country music," he told WBEE radio. Alaina earned second place. The reality show launched her singing career.

Lauren Alaina

A NEW LIFE

Like Kane, Sam was trying to start his professional music career. His new life in Nashville was just beginning. To pay his rent, he worked at a hospital, parking cars. In his free time, Sam wrote songs and performed. Many didn't know what to make of the artist. The songs he wrote didn't sound like typical country music. Some thought they sounded too much like hip-hop or R&B. At first, Sam had a hard time finding people who wanted to work with him.

GOING IT ALONE

Kane made it onto the third season of *The X Factor* in 2013. He couldn't believe it. Becoming a music star could be a reality after all. But the show's producers had a different idea about his future. They wanted him to perform as part of a boy band. It was Kane's dream to be a solo artist. He refused the offer to go on the show. Instead, he would try to make it alone.

SONGWRITERS

Many singers write their own lyrics. They might also work with songwriters. Some artists rely on songwriters completely for their music.

Songwriters write lyrics professionally. Sometimes these lyrics are for bands and solo artists. Another job is writing jingles for commercials. Others write music for songs too, not just lyrics. A lot of them collaborate with composers. These are the people who write the melodies.

Kenny Chesney

WORKING TOGETHER

Sam's path was going in a different direction. He had been working alone. It had been difficult to find people who were open-minded about his music. Then some songwriters agreed to work with him. Meeting composers Shane McAnally and Josh Osborne was an important step. The three started working on songs together. In 2012 and 2013, they had several big breakthroughs. With McAnally and Osborne, Sam wrote the song "Come Over." Kenny Chesney sang it. It became a number-one hit in 2012 for the country star.

SOCIAL MEDIA START

Kane left *The X Factor* in 2013. After that, he kept posting videos to YouTube and Facebook. They were covers of songs by country stars. Kane explained to the *Roanoke Times*, "I watched a bunch of people come up off social media, so I guess I was [kind of] hoping that it was going to work." Teaching himself the guitar was his next step. Kane woke up early to practice. He played late into the evening.

BUILDING A BAND

It was time to get serious about recording music. Sam realized he would need a band for performances and to make his first album. "I didn't know how to go about doing that," he told *Rolling Stone*. He asked his roommates to play a gig with him in Ohio. "We had such a good time, and it evolved into something more permanent," Sam noted. Later, three more friends joined his band. A childhood friend agreed to be their tour manager.

GROWING POPULARITY

Kane began posting videos in 2013. At first, they got 50 to 60 "likes." His social media presence grew slowly. Still, he was having fun. The videos d friends would show up and join him.

A cover of Lee Brice's "I Don't Dance" went viral in 2014. Kane posted the clip and went to bed. The next day, 20,000 new people were following him. On Facebook, he received 800 friend requests overnight.

Lee Brice

MIXTAPE

Sam decided to put out a mixtape of his own performances. *Between the Pines* was released for free on Facebook. This was in 2013. Not many people heard it. The album only received 79 "likes."

The next month, Billy Currington recorded a song Sam had cowritten. It was "We Are Tonight." Keith Urban's recording of "Cop Car" in 2014 also helped Sam's reputation as a songwriter. His talents were starting to get noticed.

Billy Currington

ONLINE SUCCESS

In 2015, Kane had a big hit. His cover of George Strait's "Check Yes or No" went viral. More than 7 million people watched it on Facebook.

Later that year, Kane put out a short album. *Closer* was its title. This was another success on social media. At one point after it came out, he gained 400,000 new followers on Facebook within two weeks. People were discovering Kane Brown.

GETTING SIGNED TO A RECORD LABEL

Getting a record deal isn't easy. First, musicians must practice a lot. Gigs and concerts are good ways to try out songs in front of an audience.

Preparing a demo is next. Artists make a recording of their original songs. They want it to be the best possible sample of their music.

The last step is sending the demo to record labels. Researching labels is important. Some focus on only one type of music, like country. Musicians want to make sure their songs fit with what the label wants.

STILL IN SCHOOL

More and more people were listening to Sam's songs. However, the songs were ones he had written for other artists. Performing was also a dream of his. It was hard to get signed by a record label, though. Sam decided to try something else. "I just found the cheapest way to make music and get it to people, and that was via the internet," he said in a *Rolling Stone* interview. Artists in other genres had become stars from social media. No one in country music had done it yet. But times were changing.

A DIFFERENT PATH

Many country musicians go the Nashville route. For years, this has been the traditional path to becoming a country star. Kane found success in a completely different way. People had learned about his music directly from social media. His popularity was growing. Producers were starting to pay attention. "I've had offers already, but I want to go No. 1 and make them come to me," he told the *Times Free Press* in 2015.

A LATE START

Sam got a later start in music than many other stars. In Nashville, it took a while for him to make the right connections. He didn't turn to social media until later in his music career.

Kane got famous by first covering other people's songs. Sam's fame started as other musicians performed the tracks he had written. In August 2014, Billy Currington's version of his song "We Are Tonight" hit the number-one spot. By then, Sam was ready to put out his own album.

CAREER MILESTONES

1984
Sam is born in Cedartown, Georgia.

1993
Kane is born in Chattanooga, Tennessee.

2012
Sam cowrites the hit song "Come Over" for Kenny Chesney. He wins an American Society of Composers, Authors, and Publishers award.

2013
Kane auditions successfully for *The X Factor* but doesn't compete on the show.

2014
Sam signs with MCA Nashville. In the same year, his first album, *Montevallo*, comes out.

2015
Kane's hit single "Used to Love You Sober" makes it to number two on the Country Digital Song Sales chart.

2015
Sam wins an American Music Award for New Artist of the Year.

2016
Kane signs with Sony Music Nashville. He then releases his first studio album, *Kane Brown*.

2017
Sam's hit "Body Like a Back Road" reaches number six on the Billboard Hot 100 chart. It is number one on the country list.

2018
Kane wins three American Music Awards.

CHAPTER 4

STARDOM

SONY MUSIC NASHVILLE

Many artists sign with a record label first. Then they release a hit single. Kane did the opposite. "Used to Love You Sober" came out in October 2015. A few weeks earlier, he had posted a clip on Facebook to get his fans excited. In just under three hours, the video had been viewed 1 million times. This made the record labels take notice. Sony Music Nashville signed the young artist to its label. This was in early 2016. The first move was to rerelease Kane's hit song.

MCA NASHVILLE

MCA Nashville was interested in Sam. The record label signed him in 2014. He quickly got to work with other songwriters. This time, Sam would be writing music for his own studio album.

The single "Leave the Night On" came out during the summer of 2014. Soon, it worked its way up the music charts. Eventually, it hit number 30 on the Billboard Hot 100. The single did even better on the country charts, reaching the number-one spot on two lists.

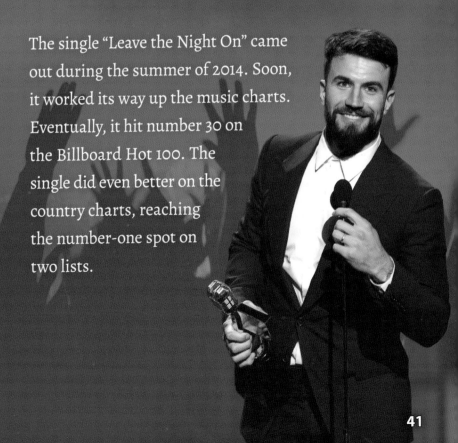

KANE BROWN

Toward the end of 2016, *Kane Brown* was released. This was Kane's debut studio album. Some songs on the album were autobiographical. "Cold Spot" and "Granddaddy's Chair" were inspired by Kane's great-grandfather. "What Ifs" was a duet with his school friend Lauren Alaina. Immediately, *Kane Brown* went to the number-one spot on the Top Country Albums chart. In 2017, it was the eighth best-selling country album of the year. The singer's success was just starting.

GRAND OLE OPRY

Every week since 1925, a radio station in Nashville has broadcast a live country music concert. The show at the Grand Ole Opry is the longest-running radio show in U.S. history. Thousands of people visit the Grand Ole Opry in Nashville every year to watch their favorite stars perform.

Singing at the Grand Ole Opry is a dream for many country artists. It is considered the home of country music. Performing there means that a musician has made it.

MONTEVALLO

In August 2014, MCA released Sam's short album called *X2C*. Only four songs were on it. Producers were trying to get everyone excited about Sam's music. The album hit number five on the Top Country Albums chart when it was released. A week after it came out, Sam performed at the Grand Ole Opry. This is one of country music's most important venues.

Sam's debut studio album, *Montevallo*, came out in October 2014. "Leave the Night On" was its lead single. The singer had also recorded his own version of "Cop Car." This song told a story about a date Sam had gone on years earlier. Much of the album was inspired by his personal life.

Grand Ole Opry

TOP OF THE CHARTS

In October 2017, Kane set a new record. He became the first artist to top five country music charts at the same time. His music reached number one on Top Country Albums, Hot Country Songs, Country Airplay, Country Digital Song Sales, and Country Streaming Songs. Sam Hunt's "Body Like a Back Road" had been number one on the Hot Country Songs list. "What Ifs" bumped it down to number two.

TOP BILLBOARD HOT 100 SINGLES

● **KANE BROWN**

#82	Used to Love You Sober		10/2015
#26	What Ifs featuring Lauren Alaina		5/2017
#15	Heaven		11/2017
#28	Lose It		6/2018

TOP ALBUM

Montevallo was a success. It sold 70,000 copies in the first week. A year later, it was nominated for a Grammy Award. Like Kane, Sam also set records. He was the second male artist to lead both Top Country Albums and Hot Country Songs with his first album. Billy Ray Cyrus was the first, 22 years earlier.

● SAM HUNT

#30	Leave the Night On	6/2014
#29	Break Up in a Small Town	9/2015
#45	Make You Miss Me	3/2016
#6	Body Like a Back Road	2/2017

FITTING IN

Kane's career was taking off. In 2018, his second album, *Experiment*, came out. On it, the musician had experimented with pop elements. Some people had a problem with his music, though. They didn't think it was really country. There were too many hip-hop and R&B elements. Kane's album wasn't nominated for any 2018 Country Music Association Awards. "I was upset a little bit just because I felt like we had a very good year," he told the Associated Press.

Hannah Lee Fowler

SOMETHING MISSING

Kane still felt like an outsider. Sam had started to feel like he was fitting in more. Things were looking up for the newly successful singer. Still, something was missing. Montevallo is the name of a town in Alabama. It's where Sam's college girlfriend Hannah Lee Fowler grew up. The couple was no longer together. But the singer missed Hannah Lee. She lived in Hawaii. In 2016, Sam decided to visit her. He hoped to win her back.

OTHER HALF

In 2017, Kane performed in Philadelphia. During the concert, he stopped singing to tell his fans some big news. "I just got engaged to a girl from Philadelphia two days ago." Earlier in the year, he had posted on social media about Katelyn Jae. "Luckily I found my other half," he wrote. The couple got married in 2018. Katelyn is also a singer. She graduated from Berklee College of Music.

Katelyn Jae

INSPIRATION

Many songs on *Montevallo* were inspired by Hannah Lee. This was no secret. In 2014, Sam talked to *E! News* about it. "A lot of the experiences I had with her and the relationship I had with her, that inspired a lot of the songwriting on the album," he said. When Sam went to Hawaii in 2016, he tried to talk Hannah Lee into coming back. It took several trips. Finally, she agreed. The pair got engaged in 2017. This was the same year as Kane and Katelyn. Later that year, Sam and Hannah got married in Cedartown, Georgia.

BIG WIN IN LOS ANGELES

Kane Brown stared straight ahead. On the drive through Los Angeles, he said almost nothing. This was the night of a big awards show. He had only been performing for a few years. Now his music had been nominated for three 2018 American Music Awards (AMAs). The singer went on to win them all. This set a record. No new artist had gone from zero to three AMAs in one year before.

AMA AWARDS

The American Music Awards are picked by fans. Some categories are open to music of all types, like Artist of the Year or Video of the Year. Others are divided into genres, such as the awards for Favorite Male Artist–Country or Favorite Song–Country. Kane won three AMAs in 2018. Sam has been nominated five times. He won the award for New Artist in 2015.

HUGE NIGHT IN NASHVILLE

Sam sat at a table, surrounded by people. Music started to play. He lifted a microphone to his mouth. The star walked through the crowd as he sang. Then he headed out onto the streets of Nashville. People cheered and took his photo.

This wasn't the reaction he had always gotten. For years, Sam struggled to make it as a country music songwriter and then singer. In 2018, he performed at the Country Music Television Awards. The crowd went wild. That showed him how far he had come.

CHAPTER 5

INFLUENCES AND COLLABORATIONS

A VARIETY OF INFLUENCES

Kane listened to all kinds of music growing up. A few of his favorite country artists are Tim McGraw, Chris Young, and Jason Aldean. In 2019, Kane toured with Aldean. His favorite music video is Sam's single "Take Your Time." He has also drawn from his love of Usher and R&B. "I had a bunch of different influences because I like a bunch of different music," he explained to *The Entertainer!* magazine.

Tim McGraw

GROWING INTEREST

Like Kane, Sam had grown up listening to mostly country music. For both, listening to R&B and rap came later. Usher was a big influence for Kane and Sam. Florida Georgia Line has inspired both artists too. This group pushed the boundaries of country music. Sam is also a fan of Taylor Swift. "She really expanded the country music appeal and the boundaries of what we can do musically," he told Taste of Country.

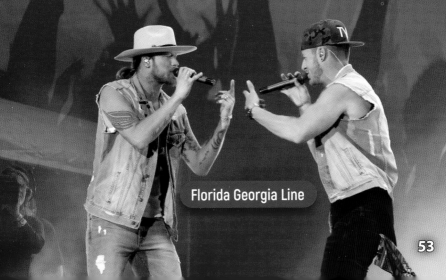

Florida Georgia Line

AUTOBIOGRAPHY

Many songs come from Kane's life experiences. "Learning" was inspired by his childhood. He sings about dealing with poverty and racism while growing up. "Cold Spot" is about his great-grandfather's store. The musician finished writing it the day Papa died. This was in 2016. It honors his memory. In 2018, Kane performed a concert wearing Papa's jacket. "I felt like he was with me," he wrote on Instagram.

MUSIC COVERS

Sam and Kane have each performed covers of the other's music, including some big hits. In 2016, Sam covered "Used to Love You Sober" at a music festival in Florida. Kane was shocked because he was a huge fan.

A year later, Kane put up an acoustic version of Sam's "Body Like a Back Road" on YouTube. The singer was a successful solo artist at this point. He still posted videos to social media to connect with his fans.

MOUNTAINS AND VALLEYS

Like Kane, Sam writes songs about his life experiences. His breakup with Hannah Lee in college inspired songs on *Montevallo*. "I used a lot of that when writing on the songs, because a lot of the songs are relationship-based," he explained to *E!* Their relationship was up and down for a while. "I probably should've included her as a cowriter on a lot of these songs," he added. Later, they got back together. Sam consulted her on music he was working on.

Hannah Lee Fowler

Lauren Alaina

WHAT IFS

One of Kane's biggest hits was the 2017 song "What Ifs."
It was from his first album. Originally, the song was
meant to be a solo. The singer and his cowriters decided
it should be a duet. Kane asked his former classmate
Lauren Alaina to sing with him. Their duet became a
number-one hit on the Hot Country Songs chart. "It's
really crazy to think we're from the same small town,
and we both used really different ways to get to this
point," Alaina said to Rare Country.

BACK ROAD

Zach Crowell was a Nashville songwriter.
However, he didn't write country music.
Instead, Crowell wrote R&B and rap music. Sam
heard some of his songs. He wanted to work with the
songwriter. One project was the mixtape *Between the
Pines*. They also cowrote "Cop Car" and "House Party."
Several songs from *Montevallo* were written with
Crowell too. The pair's biggest success came in 2017,
with "Body Like a Back Road." McAnally and Osborne
also worked on this song.

Zach Crowell

A HUGE FAN

Chris Young is one of Kane's favorite stars. He was a huge inspiration. Kane had even won his high school talent show with Young's song. In 2016, they wrote a song together. It's called "Setting the Night on Fire." "I think Chris really helped me find my voice," Kane told Taste of Country. After that duet, it was time to go on tour. He opened for Young in 2018.

COUNTRY AND HIP-HOP: "OLD TOWN ROAD"

The rapper Lil Nas X released "Old Town Road" in late 2018. The track hit number 19 on the Hot Country Songs chart. It was disqualified, though. *Billboard* decided it wasn't a true country song. They said the themes of cowboys and horses fit. However, there were too many non-country elements in the song. Listeners were surprised.

Lil Nas X then released a remix featuring country music star Billy Ray Cyrus. In 2019, the song hit number one on the Top 100 chart, which includes all kinds of music. It stayed there for 19 weeks straight. That was a new record.

DREAM TEAM

Sam's first successful collaborations
in Nashville were with the songwriters
McAnally and Osborne. "Come Over" was their first hit
together. It was for Kenny Chesney. The three went on
to write many songs for other artists. They also wrote
songs for Sam to perform.

McAnally has worked with all kinds of country stars.
He is known for writing hit songs. His songwriting has
earned him seven Grammy nominations. Sam is one of
his favorite people to work with. "It's a really unbelievable
relationship," McAnally remarked to *Rolling Stone*.

Shane McAnally

Josh Osborne

OTHER COLLABORATIONS

Kane has worked with many non-country artists. The singer reacted to people who kept telling him he wasn't country enough. "I might as well go ahead and do these songs with other artists," he told *Idolator*. In 2018, "Never Be the Same" was recorded. Pop star Camila Cabello made a remix with Kane. R&B star Khalid and Kane released a remix of "Saturday Nights" in 2019. That same year, the artist worked with Marshmello on "One Right Thing."

SURPRISE GUESTS

Country star Carrie Underwood released her album *Storyteller* in 2015. One of the songs on the album, "Heartbeat," is a duet with Sam. The next year, they performed the track together at the Grammy Awards. Sam sang with some very different artists that year too. At the 2016 Stagecoach Festival, he invited Snoop Dogg on stage with him. Pop star Bebe Rexha and rapper G-Eazy also joined him. They all sang Sam's song "House Party" for the crowd.

COMMON INFLUENCES

Kane and Sam are not typical country musicians. Both use different genres of music in their songs. They share many of the same influences. Here's a look at some of them.

Traditional Country

- "Twang" sound—nasal singing technique
- Simple melodies
- Ballads or other songs that tell stories

'90s Country

- Popular time for country music
- Shared elements with pop music
- Kane inspired by singers George Strait and Alan Jackson
- Other stars of the decade: Shania Twain, Garth Brooks, and Billy Ray Cyrus

Hip-Hop and R&B

- Rapping style of singing
- Influenced by jazz and gospel music
- Modern artists include Usher, Drake, and John Legend

STAYING POSITIVE

Some people think that country music should only sound a certain way. Modern songs have changed a lot from traditional ones. Kane isn't afraid to break the rules. Like Sam, he pushes the boundaries of what modern country sounds like. Many people are excited about the new direction Kane has taken country music. These fans remain loyal. The star said on Last.fm, "I always try to stay positive for my fans because throughout everything they have lifted me up so much."

SONGS ABOUT LIFE

Just like with Kane, some of Sam's listeners don't believe his music is true country. Sam told *Rolling Stone*, "Country music . . . has always evolved. But the one thing that has not changed is the story element. And I think country songs are truthful songs about life written by country people."

CONNECTED LIVES

Sam and Kane represent the future of country music. Each singer continues to push boundaries. They try out new sounds. Their music is the next step in a tradition that dates back over 100 years.

TAKE A LOOK INSIDE

KENDRICK LAMAR

TWO EXTRAORDINARY PEOPLE.

TRAVIS SCOTT

CHAPTER 1

EARLY LIFE

WHO IS KENDRICK LAMAR?

Kendrick Lamar is a rapper, songwriter, and producer. His full name is Kendrick Lamar Duckworth. He was born in Compton, California, on June 17, 1987. Paula and Kenny Duckworth are his parents. Three years before Kendrick was born, his parents moved to Compton from Chicago, Illinois. The couple wanted to escape violence and gangs. Compton turned out to be violent too.

WHO IS TRAVIS SCOTT?

Travis Scott is also a rapper, songwriter, and producer. Jacques Berman Webster II is his real name. On April 30, 1991, Travis was born in Houston, Texas. He comes from a mostly middle-class background. His father has a master's degree. Both of his grandfathers have advanced degrees too. The artist's parents encouraged him to get an education.